And it's Allan Ahlberg now
And he's racing away there with his pen.
The page is filling up –
and YES! a poem
One-nil to literature!

ALLAN AHLBERG

Friendly
Matches

Illustrated by Fritz Wegner

VIKING

land
14, USA
lia
Pe ada M4V 3B2
el Park,

New Delhi – 110 017, India
Penguin Books (NZ) Ltd, Cnr Rosedale and Airborne Roads, Albany,
Auckland, New Zealand
Penguin Books (South Africa) (Pty) Ltd, 5 Watkins Street, Denver Ext 4,
Johannesburg 2094, South Africa

On the World Wide Web at: www.penguin.com

Penguin Books Ltd, Registered Offices: Harmondsworth, Middlesex, England

First published 2001
1

Text copyright © Allan Ahlberg, 2001
Illustrations copyright © Fritz Wegner, 2001

The moral right of the author and illustrator has been asserted

Set in Monophoto Photina

Printed and bound in Great Britain by Butler & Tanner

British Library Cataloguing in Publication Data
A CIP catalogue record for this book is available from the British Library

ISBN 0–670–88993–8

With special thanks to:

St John's Primary School,
Essington, Wolverhampton

also

Rode Heath Primary

Brian Evans and Trevor Darby

James Yates

Church Rovers

Causeway Green Swifts

W.B.A.

Byron Thomas

Jack Sanger

and

Tony Leatherland

(it was *his* ball)

CONTENTS

So let's go out there
and show them!

Polite Children

May we have our ball, please
May we have it back?
We never meant to lose it
Or give it such a whack.

It shot right past the goalie
It shot right past the goal
And really then what happened next
Was out of our control.

It truly was such rotten luck
For all concerned that you
Were halfway up a ladder
When the ball came flying through.

We also very much regret
What happened to your cat
It's tragic when an animal
Gets landed on like that.

Your poor wife too we understand
Was pretty much upset
When phoning for the doctor
And phoning for the vet,

She quite forgot the oven.
It simply is no joke
When your husband's half unconscious
And your house is full of smoke.

The fire-brigade, of course, meant well
It wasn't their mistake
That there was no fire to speak of
Just a bit of well-done steak.

Still clouds have silver linings
And pains are soon forgot
While your lawn will surely flourish
From the hosing that it got.

The game of life is never lost
The future's not all black
And the ball itself seems quite unmarked.
So . . . may we have it back?

Talk Us Through It, Charlotte

Well I shouldn't't've been playin' really
Only there to watch me brother.
My friend fancies his friend, y'know.
Anyway they was a man short.

Stay out on the wing, they said
Give 'em something to think about.
So I did that for about an hour;
Never passed to me or anything.

The ball kind of rebounded to me.
I thought, I'll have a little run with it.
I mean, they wasn't passin' to me
Was they? So off I went.

I ran past this first boy
He sort of fell over.
It was a bit slippery on that grass
I will say that for him.

Two more of 'em come at me
Only they sort of tackled each other
Collided – arh.* I kept going.
There was this great big fat boy.

One way or another I kicked it
Through his legs and run round him.
That took a time. Me brother
Was shouting, Pass it to me, like.

Well like I said, I'd been there an hour.
They never give *me* a pass
Never even spoke to me
Or anything. So I kept going.

Beat this other boy somehow
Then there was just the goalie.
Out he came, spreadin' himself
As they say. I was really worried.

I thought he was going to hug me.
So I dipped me shoulder like they do
And the goalie moved one way, y'know
And I slammed it in the net.

Turned out afterwards it was the winner.
The manager said I was very good.
He wants me down at trainin' on Tuesday.
My friend says she's comin' as well.

Surely This Boy Must Play for England

In an ordinary house in an ordinary room
In an ordinary single bed
An ordinary boy in pyjamas
Flicks a casual goal with his head.

Surely this boy must play for England.

Helps his dad after breakfast
To wash and polish the car
Beats his man in the garage
And hammers one in off the bar.

It's madness – he's only ten.

Helps his mum in the afternoon
With the supermarket trip
While clearing a wall of shoppers
With a David Beckham chip.

If he's good enough, he's old enough.

Plays with his little sister
Takes the dog for a stroll
And dumbfounds the local pigeons
With an unbelievable goal.

Ten-year-old makes the squad.

Eats his tea in the evening
Talks to his gran on the phone
Faces four giant defenders
And takes them on on his own.

Surely this boy *must* play for England.

Cleans his teeth in the bathroom
Draws in the steamy glass
Shuffles his feet on the bathroom mat
And flicks a casual pass.

Youngest-ever sub takes the field.

In an ordinary house in an ordinary room
In an ordinary single bed
An ordinary boy plays for England
And stands the game on its head.

A hat-trick, and he's still only ten.

Leaves the ground with the match ball
While his mother tidies the pitch
And his dad turns off the floodlights
With a casual flick of the switch.

They think it's all over.

Just an ordinary boy in pyjamas
Fast asleep at the end of the day
Though his feet still twitch in the darkness
And he's never too tired . . . to play.

Dad on the Line
(or a boy's nightmare)

I'm playing in this big game
New kit, great pitch
Proper goals with proper nets.

All of a sudden
With rattle and scarf
And a flask of tea . . . there' s Dad.

Come on, my son! says Dad
Square ball! says Dad
We are the champions! says Dad
Que sera, sera.

*

I'm playing now in a bigger game
Brand new ball, managers in dugouts
Proper linesmen and a proper ref.

All of a sudden
With our dog on a lead
And a meat pie . . . there's Dad.

Come on you reds! says Dad
Up the Rovers! says Dad
We're going to Wem-b-ley! says Dad
Que sera, sera.

*

And now the biggest game of all
Changing rooms with sunken baths
Proper turnstiles and a proper stand.

All of a sudden
With his mates from work
And a giant photograph of me . . . there's Dad.

Offside! says Dad
Foul! says Dad
That's my lad out there! says Dad
Que sera, sera.

Then, usually at this point
He runs onto the pitch.
The stewards chase him
(He's still got the giant photo)
The crowd goes mad
The ref stares accusingly at me . . .

And I wake up.

Friendly Matches

In friendly matches
Players exchange pleasantries
Hallo, George!
How's the Missus?
Admire opponents' kit
Smart shirt, Bert!
Sympathize with linesmen
Difficult decision, there.
And share their half-time oranges.

In friendly matches
Players apologize for heavy tackles
How clumsy of me.
And offer assistance with throw-ins
Allow us to help you with that heavy ball.

In friendly matches
Players and substitutes alike
Speak well of referees
First-rate official
Sound knowledge of the game
Excellent eyesight!

In friendly matches
Players celebrate opposing players' birthdays
With corner-flag candles
On pitch-shaped cakes.

In friendly matches
Players take it in turns
No, no, please, after *you*

to score.

You are absolutely right. That was unforgivable!

Lullaby for a Referee's Baby

The pitch is cold and dark
The night is dark and deep
The players all have gone to bed
So sleep, baby, sleep.

The whistle's on the shelf
The boots are in a heap
The kit is in the laundry bag
So sleep, baby, sleep.

The house is warm and dark
The stairs are dark and steep
And Daddy's here beside your cot
To send you off . . . to sleep.

Mr Bloor

There was a man named Mr Bloor
Who liked to referee *and* score.

He'd blow his whistle, swing his boot
Beat half a dozen boys – and shoot.

(He was a teacher in our school
His favourite team was Liverpool.)

He also loved to commentate
'Bloor's got the ball – Bloor's going great!

He's beat his man, what rare control
He's round the full back now and – GOAL!

His legs are strong, his brain is quick!'
(Sometimes he'd let *us* have a kick.)

But Mr Bloor the referee
Was also fair, as you will see.

He'd score a goal and strut with pride
Then stop and rule himself offside.

He'd cover back and tackle hard
Yet give himself a yellow card,

Bulldoze boys caught in his path
And send himself for an early bath.

On rare occasions I recall
Our Mr Bloor would *pass* the ball.

Leaving some kid, like Vinny Cole
(Who never scored), with an open goal.

'It's Vinny now, all full of dinner
Dazzling footwork and – the winner!'

Mr Bloor was short and wide
He played with trousers tucked inside

His ordinary socks and on his head
He wore a bobble hat, bright red.

Sometimes his girlfriend, Miss Levine
(She taught us too), would run the line.

She'd stand there smiling, tall and slim
And wave her little flag at him.

Eventually his knees gave way
And doctors said he shouldn't play.

Now Mr Bloor's a mere spectator
Oh yes of course *and* commentator.

'He's got the ball, what sweet control
Deceives the goalie now and – GOAL!'

Team Talk

Marcus, don't argue with the ref.
Yes, he needs glasses
Yes, he should keep up with the play
Yes, yes, he's a pawn
In some international betting syndicate
But *don't argue with him.*
He'll send you off.
And if he doesn't, I will.

Billy, you're the goalie – right?
Listen, you're *allowed* to use your hands
OK?
It's in the rules
It's legal.

Another thing
What's that you've got in the back of the net?
That carrier bag
I've seen it – what is it?
Hm.
Well, leave-it-a-lone
You can eat later.

Now then, Michael
You've got Charles outside you, OK?
Unmarked, OK?
I know he's only your brother
But pass to him.

Marcus, another thing
Don't argue with the linesman either
Or me, for that matter
Or *anybody*
Just –
Just –
Just –
Marcus . . . shut up.

Kevin, a word.
Their number seven
You're supposed to be marking him
And he's scored five already, right?
Well that's . . . enough
Close him down.

So come on lads
The golden rules – remember?
Hold your positions
Run into space
Call for the ball
Play to the whistle
Pass only to members of your own team.

Last of all
NEVER GIVE UP
Thirteen – nil
Sounds bad, but it's not the end.
We can turn it round
We can get a result
It's a game of two halves.

So let's go out there –
And show 'em!

Billy . . . are you eating?

Soccer Sonnet

Now children, said the teacher with a smile
Put down your books and let your pencils fall
Come out into the playground for a while
And run around with me and kick a ball.
We'll pick two teams and use our coats for goals
(But leave our bags and worries at the door)
And play the game with all our hearts and souls
And never mind the weather or the score.
I'll promise not to test your soccer skills
The ball's the only thing you'll need to pass
There'll be no Key Stage Three or spelling drills
There'll be no top or bottom of the class.
So let's forget the gold stars for a day
And get outside – and run around – and play.

Team Talk 2
(the next match)

Marcus, what did I say?

I warned you

You're *argumentative*

He was bound to send you off

Your own mother would send you off.

And besides –

Besides –

Besides –

Marcus . . . shut up.

Dominic, a word.

Mud.

Stop worrying about it, OK?

There's no prize for the cleanest pair of shorts

Never mind what your auntie says

Get stuck in.

No, Jonathan, that old fella on the line

Is *not* a scout for Man. United.

No.

No, he isn't.

Don't ask me how I know

I just do.

Call it instinct.

Come here, you two

Michael – this is Charles

Charles – this is Michael

Say, Hallo.

Say, Pleased to meet you.

I *mean* it.

Now *pass* to each other.

Billy, empty your pockets
All of 'em.
What's this?
Goalkeeping's an art, Billy
It's vital
The last line of defence
You have to *concentrate*
And how can you expect to do that
With a pocketful of peanuts?
Get rid of 'em.

How many shirts are you wearing,
Craig – hm?
It's not that cold
You look like . . .
No, not *me*, Marcus
You look like – well, never mind.

Brian, brilliant header.
Unstoppable.
Now let's see if you can do it again
At their end.

Yes, and another thing
I know your dad's an expert
I can hear him
We can all hear him
But take no notice – right?
If I'd wanted you to play through the middle
I would not have picked you
At left back.

So let's get out there
Keep plugging away
They're not eight goals better than us
Anyway ten men are sometimes harder to beat
Than a full team. Right?

And remember *Golden Rules*
NEVER-GIVE-UP.

Billy . . . is that a biscuit?
Mmm. Just what I need.

The Match (c. 1950)

The match was played in Albert Park
From half-past four till after dark
By two opposing tribes of boys
Who specialized in mud and noise;

Scratches got from climbing trees
Runny noses, scabby knees
Hair shaved halfway up the head
And names like Horace, Archie, Ted.

The match was played come rain or shine
By boys who you could not confine
Whose common goals all unconcealed
Were played out on the football field.

Off from school in all directions
Sparks of boys with bright complexions
Rushing home with one idea
To grab their boots . . . and disappear.

But mother in the doorway leaning
Brings to this scene a different meaning
The jobs and duties of a son
Yes, there are *errands to be run.*

Take this wool to Mrs Draper
Stop at Pollock's for a paper
Mind this baby, beat this rug
Give your poor old mum a hug.

Eat this apple, eat this cake
Eat these dumplings, carrots, steak!
Bread 'n' drippin', bread 'n' jam
Mind the traffic, so long, scram.

Picture this, you're gazing down
Upon that smoky factory town.
Weaves of streets spread out, converge
And from the houses boys emerge.

Specks of boys, a broad selection
Heading off in one direction
Pulled by some magnetic itch
Up to the park, onto the pitch.

Boys in boots and boys in wellies
Skinny boys and boys with bellies
Tiny boys with untied laces
Brainy boys with violin cases.

The match was played to certain rules
By boys from certain streets and schools
Who since their babyhood had known
Which patch of earth to call their own.

The pitch, meanwhile, you'd have to say
Was nothing, just a place to play.
No nets, no posts, no *lines*, alas
The only thing it had was grass.

Each team would somehow pick itself
No boys were left upon the shelf
No substitutions, sulks or shame
If you showed up, you got a game.

Not 2·3·5 or 4·2·4
But 2·8·12 or even more.
Six centre forwards, five right wings
Was just the normal run of things.

Lined up then in such formations
Careless of life's complications
Deaf to birdsong, blind to flowers
Prepared to chase a ball for hours,

A swarm of boys who heart and soul
Must make a bee-line for the goal.
A kind of ordered anarchy
(There was, of course, *no* referee).

They ran and shouted, ran and shot
(At passing they were not so hot)
Pulled a sock up, rolled a sleeve
And scored more goals than you'd believe.

Slid and tackled, leapt and fell
Dodged and dribbled, dived as well
Headed, shouldered, elbowed, kneed
And, half-time in the bushes, peed.

With muddy shorts and muddy faces
Bloody knees and busted laces
Ruddy cheeks and plastered hair
And voices buffeting the air.

Voices flung above the trees
Heard half a mile away with ease,
For every throw in, every kick
Required an inquest double quick.

A shouting match, all fuss and fury
(Prosecutors, judges, jury)
A match of mouths set to repeat
The main and muddier match of feet.

Thus hot and bothered, loud and nifty
That's how we played in 1950
A maze of moves, a fugue of noise
From forty little boiling boys.

Yet there was talent, don't forget
Grace and courage too, you bet
Boys like Briggs or Tommy Gray
Who were, quite simply, *born* to play.

You could have stuck them on the moon
They would have started scoring soon
No swanky kit, uncoached, unheeded
A pumped-up ball was all they needed.

Around the fringes of the match
Spectators to this hectic patch
Younger sisters, older brothers
Tied-up dogs and irate mothers.

A mother come to claim her twins
(Required to *play* those violins).
A little sister, Annabelle,
Bribed with a lolly not to tell.

Dogs named Rover, Rex or Roy
Each watching one particular boy.
A pup mad keen to chase the ball
The older dogs had seen it all.

The match was played till after dark
(Till gates were closed on Albert Park)
By shadowy boys whose shapes dissolved
Into the earth as it revolved.

Ghostly boys who flitted by
Like bats across the evening sky,
A final fling, a final call
Pursuing the invisible ball.

The match was played, the match *is* over
For Horace, Annabelle and Rover.
A multitude of feet retrace
The steps that brought them to this place.

For gangs of neighbours, brothers, friends
A slow walk home is how it ends,
Into a kitchen's steamy muddle
To get a shouting at . . . or cuddle.

See it now, you're looking down
Upon that lamp-lit factory town.
It's late (it's *night*) for Rex or Ted
And everybody's gone to bed.

Under the rooftops slicked with rain
The match is being played again
By two opposing well-scrubbed teams
Who race and holler in their dreams.

The Song of the Sub

I'm standing on the touchline
In my substitute's kit
As though it doesn't matter
And I don't mind a bit.

I'm trying to be patient
Trying not to hope
That my friends play badly
And the team can't cope.

I'm a sub, I'm a sub and I sing this song
And I'm only ever wanted when things go wrong.

When a boy has the measles
When a boy goes lame
The teacher turns to me
And I get a game.

When a boy gets kicked
Or shows up late
And they need another player
I'm the candidate.

I'm a sub, I'm a sub and I sing this song
And I'm only ever wanted when things go wrong.

I warm up on the touchline
I stretch and bend
And wonder what disasters
My luck will send.

If a boy got lost
Or ran away to France
If a boy got *kidnapped*
Would I get my chance?

I'm a sub, I'm a sub and I sing this song
And I'm only ever wanted when things go wrong.

I feel a bit embarrassed
That I'm not bothered more
When decisions go against us
And the other teams score.

I try to keep my spirits up
I juggle with the ball
And hope to catch the teacher's eye
It does no good at all.

Just a sub, just a sub till my dying day
And I only get a kick when the others can't play.

*

I'm standing on the touchline
On the very same spot
And it *does* really matter
And I *do* mind – a lot.

I think I'll hang my boots up
It's not the game for me
Then suddenly I hear those words:
You're on! I am? *Yippee!*

The Grey Boys

Oh Mother may I go to play
With the grey boys in the street
For I hear the thud of a booted ball
And the clattering of feet.

My window overlooks the street
The street lamps light the game
The boys are mad to kick the ball
And I feel just the same.

A yellow haze hangs round the lamps
Under the smoky sky
And up and down the clattery street
The shadowy boys go by.

Oh Mother may I join the game
With the grey boys of the town
For I feel much better than I did
And my temperature is down.

My fevered brow is cooler now
My pulse is calm and slow
My hands lie still upon the quilt
Oh Mother . . . may I go?

How to Score Goals

(1)

Approach with ball
Point left
Say, 'Ooh, look – a bunny rabbit!'
Shoot right
Goal.

(2)

Approach with ball
Point right
Say, 'Ooh, look – a fiver!'
Shoot left
Goal.

(3)

Approach with ball
Say, 'Sorry about all this trickery
I never saw any rabbit'
Offer to shake hands
Shoot.

(4)

Approach with ball

Sudden sound of bagpipes

(For this you will need an accomplice)

Goal.

(5)

Approach with ball

Plus cake

Sing 'Happy Birthday to you!'

Invite goalie

To blow his candles out

etc.

(6)

Approach with ball

Point skywards

Say, 'Ooh, look – a vulture!'

(He will have forgotten the rabbit by this time)

Goal.

(7)

Approach with ball

Say, 'I bet I can hit you with this next shot'

Shoot.

(8)

Approach with ball

Say, 'I am being sponsored for charity

A pound for every goal I score'

Shoot

Shoot

Shoot.

(9)

Approach with ball
Say, 'Smart boots you've got there
Very smart
Not like these old things of mine
Still, Dad'll get a job soon
Then
When Mum comes out of hospital
And the baby's had his – '
Shoot.

(10)

Approach with ball
Sudden eclipse of sun
(For this you will need to consult astronomical charts)
Goal.

(11)

Approach with ball
Think of something . . .
Goal.

Elephants v. Insects

The Elephants and the Insects
Came out to play a match
They trampled in the jungle
Till they'd cleared a little patch.
They scuttled round and trumpeted
Just glad to be alive
Until the half-time whistle
When the score was 15–5.

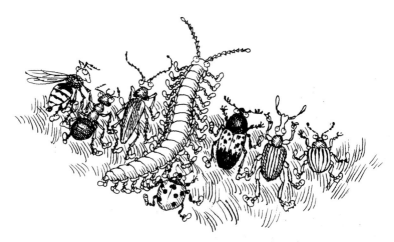

The Insects in the second half
Brought on a substitute
A modest little centipede
But brother could he shoot.
He ran around on all his legs
Beneath the tropic sun
And by the time he'd finished
Well, the Insects they had won.

Oh tell us, said the Elephants
We're mystified indeed
Why wait until the second half
To play the centipede?
That's easy, cried the Insects
As they carried off the cup
He needs an hour to sort his boots
And tie his laces up!

Creating Space

What is he doing that boy in midfield
With the innocent-looking face?
He's losing himself in the midst of a crowd
Creating space.

How does he do it that ordinary boy
With no obvious surge of pace,
Find for himself on the crowded pitch
A private place?

The rest of the team and the other team too
Are happy to tackle and chase.
He strolls by himself in the midst of the crowd
Creating space.

Where has he gone to that ghost of a boy
With the unastonishing face?
How could he shift from the well-marked pitch
Without a trace?

The rest of the team and the other team too
Continue to tackle and chase.
He's off on his own in a bubble of time
Creating space.

Soccer's Strangest Match

It was the strangest match I ever saw.
Take the final score for instance,
Five-all – and one player got all ten of them,
With his head.
How often do you see that?

And the weather – unbelievable.
At the kick-off it was so cold
Half the players had overcoats on
Gloves and scarves – balaclavas.
Pretty soon one of the goalkeepers had a small fire
    going
In the back of his goal.
(Nothing in the rules apparently to prevent that.)

Then there was the inflatable goalie.
Under *his* overcoat, it turned out
He had some kind of rubber suit.
His manager was pumping him up from the touchline
Slowly, imperceptibly he hoped, to avoid suspicion.
After a while though this goalie was just lying there
Sideways
His head propped up on his hand
Filling the goal.
Whereupon of course the opposition protested.

Meanwhile at regular intervals
And both ends
The amazing sequence of headers was going in.

The pitch had its peculiarities too.
A public footpath ran diagonally across it.
Stubborn old men with newspapers and dogs
Wandered casually in and out of the game.
A young mother in a hurry
With her baby in a pushchair
And concerned for her offspring's safety
Kicked savagely at the ball.
Luckily she failed to score.
(There's not much in the rules about *that*.)

The weather was beginning to fluctuate wildly.

There was a tremendous, freakish storm of hailstones.

The temperature rose thirty degrees.

The pitch, the players, the ball, the referee,

Linesmen, spectators

All were steaming, like hot pans on a stove.

Briefly the fog was so bad

Substitutes were coming onto the field unnoticed.

The goals continued to mount up.
The weather continued to amaze:
Phenomenal rainbows now
So brightly arrayed around one goal
As to create an almost religious effect.
It was into this blaze of light
That the goal-scorer headed his finest (own) goal
A thunderous effort that came back off the bar
And caught him again on the side of the head
As he was turning away,
Rebounding instantly
Beyond the irate and rainbow-hued keeper.

Meanwhile at the other end
The manager of the previously inflated goalie
Was still up to his tricks
This time – stilts.
The goalie
When his manager had done with him
Towered absurdly above his own crossbar.

Another remarkable feature of this game
Was its duration.
It lasted, half-time included
For four and a half hours.
The referee's watch
Indeed all watches within a mile radius
Had been affected it seems
By the outlandish weather conditions.

So the players as you can imagine
Were dropping with exhaustion
When the final whistle blew.
Even so each team raised a cheer
For their sporting opponents
And *both* teams
Every last man and nun –
I forgot to mention her –
Summoned up the energy and grace
To carry the ten-goal hero from the field.
How often do you see *that?*

By the way, another thing I forgot
It was a cup match.
Yes . . .
A week later
They had it all to do again.

The Footballer's Love of the Ball

Grab the ball and boot it high
See it going up the sky
See it falling down and then
Boot it straight back up again.

Boot it high and boot it higher
Boot it almost out of sight
Send it shooting up at teatime
See it tumbling back at night.

See it rise and see it fall
Earth to sky and ball to ball.

Who Kicked Cock Robin?

Not I said the owl
Gazing down sleepy-eyed
I'm not that kind of fowl
And we're on the same side.

Not I said the bee
Buzzing back to his hive
Cock Robin kicked me
And then took a dive.

Not I said the grub
My excuse is complete
I was only a sub
And – I ain't got no feet.

The Song of the Referee

When the teams are yelling
And you can't think what to do
Blow a little whistle
Blow a little whistle.
When the crowd goes crazy
And the one they hate is you
Blow a little whistle
Blow a little whistle.

Keep your spirits high
Look your troubles in the eye
And when times are hard
Show your woes the yellow card.

When the teams are snarling
Like a pack of carnivores
Blow a little whistle
Blow a little whistle.
When the crowd is baying
And the blood they want is yours
Blow a little whistle
Blow a little whistle.

Smile away that frown
Never let it get you down
Raise your glass and raise a laugh
Give those griefs an early bath.

When you're homeward bound and find
Some blighter's pinched your coat
Blow a little whistle
Blow a little whistle.
When upon your windscreen
There's a traffic warden's note
Blow a little whistle
Blow a little whistle.

There's more to life than this
Give your wife a kiss
Grab the baby, feed the cat
Phone your old mum for a chat
You're a part of all their plans
Yes! Even referees have fans

And blow a little whistle.

My Favourite Goal

Not Beckham's astonishing long-range chip
From the halfway line v. Wimbledon.
Nor Carlisle's *goalie's* winner
(His name was Jimmy Glass)
Last match of the season
In added time, ninety-fifth minute
All twenty-two players in Plymouth's half
Saving his side from relegation.
His own comment: It fell to me,
Wallop, goal, thank you very much.

Not Bergkamp's perfect strike
High ball dropping over his shoulder
For Holland in '98 v. Argentina,
Nor even one of my own rare efforts.
No, no, *my* favourite goal
Was scored at the City Ground
29th November 1989
By a little Nottingham Forest winger
Named Gary Crosby.
And me a West Bromwich Albion man.

An attack had broken down.
Man. City's keeper had the ball
Preparing to launch it upfield.
Crosby came nipping in behind him
Unobtrusively, on tip toe it seemed (Sh!)
And *headed* it, neatly
Clean as a whistle (no whistle)
Off the flat of that flabbergasted goalie's hand
Held out like an attentive waiter's tray
And tapped it in the net.

A lovely goal, the charm of it, yes
The wit of it. Thank you very much.

Dream Football

Dream football is the harder game
The grass is devilishly long
And growing
Fish appear in the trainer's bucket
Your mother has set up a small shop
On the halfway line
You are obliged to play in your underpants.

The Famous Five-a-Side

The early morning sun beams bright
Into our uncle's cottage kitchen.
Uncle himself researches in his study,
Our parents are conveniently absent.

We breakfast well on eggs and toast
Get changed into our freshly-laundered kit
Pick apples in the sunny orchard
Pack boots and buns and lemonade.

The village street is oddly quiet
Anxious faces at the bread-shop window.
There is a rumour of strange goings-on
Burglaries . . . a missing necklace.

The pitch upon the village green
Still sparkles with its morning dew
Except that is for one mysterious patch.
We fasten Timmy's dog-lead to a bench.

Descending from a battered van
The opposing team are not what we expect.
Older and scowling, oddly kitted out
Their goalie has an eye-patch and a beard.

The ref too has a sinister air
Arriving out of breath and with a limp.
He keeps the ball clutched closely to his chest
And seems unwilling to relax his grip.

'This lot aren't Barford Rovers, that's for sure,'
We whisper as we line up on the pitch.
Julian pretends to tie a bootlace up
And tells the rest of us he's got a plan.

The game begins. Their strategy is odd.
They crowd around the ball and hardly move.
The referee limps slowly up and down.
The bearded goalie smokes a cigarette.

Then suddenly we hear a sound
A hollow croaking voice *beneath* the grass.
A trap-door in the turf begins to rise
And reaching up around it comes . . . a hand!

George boots the ball now high into the air
It ends up in the smoking goalie's net.
His team mates oddly chase it in,
The hobbling referee not far behind.

'This is our chance, chaps!' Julian cries.
We charge then at the crowded goal,
Unhook the net and drop it on them all:
The spurious players and the bogus ref.

Meanwhile up from his dungeon cell
One plain-clothes CID man stumbles forth.
'Well done you fellows – excellent!' he gasps.
(This was more 'undercover' than he'd planned.)

'This is the Melford Mob,' he says.
'Been on their trail all year.
I shouldn't doubt there'll be a big reward.'
'We *knew* they were suspicious,' George declares.

Another van appears: the Black Maria.
The losing side are bundled in.
'You blasted kids!' the captured goalie growls.
Brave Timmy barks as they are driven off.

That little dog now trots towards the ball,
He sniffs and scrabbles at it with his paws.
'He wants to tell us something,' Anne explains.
Yes – have you guessed? – the *necklace* was inside.

Back home to Uncle's cottage, time for lunch.
There's sausages and chocolate cake and squash.
'Good game?' says Uncle, peering round the door.
'Oh absolutely yes!' cries George. 'We won!'

May Pitches

In the long-shadowed evenings
Final games are played
On rutted dusty pitches
Worn down in places to baked mud
With daisies and dandelions
And new grass greening the wings.
Flaked paint on the goalposts
Fossilized stud marks in the ground
Rapidly fading touchlines.

Close by, secure within a frame of ropes
A fresh flat cosseted square
Awaits its turn.
The last offside hangs in the air
A cuckoo from a long way off cuckoos
And farther still and fainter
The first howzat.

1966, *or* *Were You There, Daddy?*

In the fabulous year of '66
The year beyond compare
When England carried off the cup
Dear Daddy, were you there?

Yes, my son, I was there.

When Bobby Charlton ran midfield
And Hurst leapt in the air
And Peters drifted down the wing
Dear Daddy, were you there?

Yes, my son, absolutely.

When Nobby Stiles snapped at their heels
And Wilson played it square
And Gordon Banks was flying
Dear Daddy, were you there?

Yes, my son, no question.

When Bobby Moore was in control
And Ball was everywhere
And Beckenbauer was trouble
Dear Daddy, were you there?

Yes, my son, I really was.

When England carried off the cup
And anthems filled the air
And Wembley was the place to be
Dear Daddy, were *you* there?

Oh yes, my son, oh yes, oh yes
Oh yes I was *really* there.
When Bobby Charlton ran midfield
And Peters played it square
And big Jack Charlton headed out
And Hunt was everywhere
And Cohen tackled like a tank
And Beckenbauer showed flair
And Gordon Banks was flying . . .

       flying
Your dad, Oh-he-was-there!

The Lovely Ball of Leather

About a mile North of Preston
On a cool November day
A team of boys plus substitutes
Was setting off to play.
They sat there in the minibus
Just gazing straight ahead
Listening to their manager
And this is what he said.

O boys, he cried, O fellas
I couldn't ask for more
You run your little socks off
Though you never seem to score.
But I know you'll keep on trying
You'll strive and strain and sweat
Till that lovely ball of leather
Goes flying in the net.

Just a little West of Bromwich
In the January rain
That selfsame team of players
Was on the road again.
They crowded in the minibus
As it carried them away
While their manager-cum-driver
Had these quiet words to say.

O boys, he cried, O fellas
I've got this rotten cold
My knee's a bit arthritic
And I'm really rather old.
But I know I will recover
My life's not over yet
Till that lovely ball of leather
Goes flying in the net.

In a lay-by South of Hampton
On a balmy April night
When the road was dark and empty
And the sky was starry bright,
A team of boys plus substitutes
Was sitting in the bus
Eating chips and burgers
While their manager spoke thus.

O boys, he cried, O fellas
I *knew* that you could play
I knew the gods were with us
And we'd get a goal some day.
It was a precious moment
Which I never will forget
When that lovely ball of leather
Went flying in the net.

The Betsy Street Booters

We are the Betsy Street Booters
We are the girls you can't beat
The sharpest and straightest of shooters
On twenty-two talented feet.

The boys in our school think we're clueless
Which just shows how little they know
We played them last week in the playground
And beat them five times in a row.

The boys say our tactics are rubbish
Soccer skills nought out of ten
We played them once more on a real pitch
And beat them all over again.

The boys in our school blame the weather
The bounce and a bad referee
We played them in glorious sunshine
And hammered them 17–3.

The boys now appear quite disheartened
And wonder just what they should do
They're talking of taking up netball . . .
But we're pretty good at that too.

We are the Betsy Street Booters
We are the girls you can't beat
The sharpest and straightest of shooters
On twenty-two talented feet.

Team Talk 14

Lads, believe me
You know it
I know it
We are not the best team
In this league
But this lot –
Marcus, are you listening?
This lot
I have to say it –
Are worse!

Believe me
We can beat 'em
What am I saying –
We *are* beating 'em!
Yippee!

So this is the situation, lads

Stay calm

Stay focused

Get out there –

Yes, *now* Billy –

Get out there

And whatever it was you were doing –

This is the plan, right Michael?

Right Charles?

What*ever* it *was* you were *doing*

Keep doing it.

OK?

The Goals of Bingo Boot

The fans in the stands are silent
You could hear the fall of a pin
For the fabulous game just ended
And the tale that's about to begin.

In nineteen hundred and twenty-two
A little boy was born
His baby cot was second-hand
His baby shawl was torn.
He had no teeth or teddy bear
His hair was incomplete
But he was the possessor of
The most amazing feet.

When Bingo Boot was two years old
He chewed his little crust
His poor old dad was on the dole
His poor old pram was bust.
Yet Bingo wasn't worried
Though his baby feet would itch
And he could hardly wait till
He could stroll – out on the pitch.

In school young Bingo languished
At the bottom of the class
His ball control was good
It was exams he couldn't pass.
His little pals all shouted, 'Foul!'
And tended to agree
If only teachers tested feet
He'd get a Ph.D.

And all the while in streets and parks
On pitches large or small
Without a proper pair of boots
Sometimes without a ball!
With tin cans in the clattering yard
In weather cold or hot
Young Bingo shimmied left and right
And scored with every shot.

His poor old mum scrubbed office floors
His poor old gran did too
The pantry was an empty place
The rent was overdue.
Then Bingo had a brainwave
Shall I tell you what he did?
He sold himself to the Arsenal
For thirteen thousand quid.

The first game that he ever played
At the tender age of ten
Young Bingo just ran rings round
Eleven baffled men.
The fans of course went crazy
The fans went, 'Ooh!' and 'Ah!'
While Bingo took the match ball home
And bought his dad a car.

And so the years went flying by
In liniment and sweat
Life was a great high-scoring game
An ever-bulging net
And Arsenal won the cup and league
Six seasons on the trot
All on account of Bingo Boot
And his most amazing shot.

But now the storm clouds gathered
And at last the whistle blew
For the start of a really *crucial* game
The battle of World War Two.
It was England versus Germany
And Bingo heard the call
He marched away in his shooting boots
To assist in Adolf's fall.

Then when the war was finished
And he'd left the fusiliers
Brave Bingo served the Gunners
For another fifteen years.
No net was ever empty
No sheet was ever clean
He scored more goals a season
Than even Dixie Dean.

His goals in life were modest though
He had no wish to be
Sir Bingo Boot of Camden Town
Or Bingo O. B. E.
He loved his wife and family
His kiddies, Joyce and Jim,
He never went to see the King
The King came to see him.

His twilight years were mostly spent
With a ball in the local park
Kicking about with the local team
Having a laugh and a lark.
Yet still they couldn't stop him
His old swerve worked a treat
Till he died at last with his boots on
Those most amazing feet.

Eyes down for Bingo (in his grave)
The final whistle blown
The fans rolled up from miles around
'You'll never walk alone!'
While Bingo's spirit shimmied
With all its usual grace
And then was . . . relegated
To a most appalling place.

...I've pulled a few strings
I must confess
To arrange your
Transfer here!

The Devil sat in his chairman's chair
And spoke in Bingo's ear
'I've pulled a few strings, I must confess
To arrange your transfer here.
For we've got this little match, y'see
(And I've got this little bet)
Away to the Heavenly City
And we've never beaten them yet.'

The Heavenly City were quite a side
(With fans who could *really* sing)
Cherubs and seraphs in the squad
And angels on the wing.
St Paul was a rock at centre half
St Elvis a rock 'n' roll
They had Mother Teresa to captain the team
And Almighty God in goal.

The kick-off time was three o'clock
At the City's heavenly ground
The angels of the Lord came down
And passed the ball around.
The tackles started flying
Nero fouled a nun
And the ref booked Good King Wenceslas
For a trip on Attila the Hun.

The Hades fans were howling
'We're the boys from Beelzebub!'
While God took Charlie Chaplin off
And brought Jesus on as a sub.
The second half went racing by
The pace was faster still
There was less than a minute left to play
And the score remained nil-nil.

Then Bingo dribbled round St Mark
Who never had a prayer
Left frail St Francis on his knees
And danced past Fred Astaire.
The goal was at his mercy now
It seemed he couldn't fail
When – bang! – a tackle from behind
From Florence Nightingale.

A penalty! The crowd was stunned.
The Devil's lot gave thanks,
Though God in goal, the angels cried,
Was as good as Gordon Banks.
A cruel choice for Bingo
Whatever should he do
Be false to his god-given gifts
Or give the Devil his due?

Even God had a frown on His face
And powerful reasons to pray.
If I let this in, He told himself
There'll be the Devil to pay.
Now Bingo stepped up with the ball
And placed it on the spot
Stepped back, breathed deep, ran calmly in
Then shimmied left . . . and shot.

*

In nineteen hundred and twenty-two
A little boy was born
His baby cot was second-hand
His baby shawl was torn.
Who would have guessed that at the end
This tiny tot would be
The one who beat Almighty God
With the perfect penalty?

No goalie could have saved that shot
No God or Holy Ghost
But it went where Bingo placed it
And hit the holy post,
Rebounded like a rocket
To Marie Antoinette
Who skipped up to the other end
And slammed it in the net.

The fans in the stands went barmy
City had won one-nil.
The Devil stayed down in his dugout
Defeat was a bitter pill.
Till God came along with an offer
Quite genuine and real
To forget their bet and agree instead
On a little . . . transfer deal.

So Bingo rose to Heaven
Up to the Pearly Gate.
'The boy done good!' St Peter cried
'The boy done great!'
And there he lives . . . forever
His goals in life complete
That sainted soccer player
With the most amazing feet.

The fans in the stands are leaving
As fast as their wings will allow
They think that the story's over
            It is now.

Allan Ahlberg & Fritz Wegner

What a team!

PLEASE MRS BUTLER
The most important 20th century
children's poetry book
- *Books for Keeps* poll

HEARD IT IN THE PLAYGROUND
The second most important 20th century
children's poetry book
- *Books for Keeps* poll

Combined sales of over a million copies!

wow!